# ATHENS

ANCIENT - BYZANTINE - MODERN CITY
MUSEUMS

*EDITIONS G. GOUVOUSSIS*
*5 RATZIERI STR. 117 42*
*ATHENS - GREECE*

# ATHENS

At sunset the mountains encircling Athens turn a miraculously transparent purple which radiates over the waters of the Saronic Gulf to the distant chains of the Peloponnese rising behind the triangular peak of Aegina. No wonder the violet-crowned has been envied by gods and men ever since Poseidon and Athena disputed the patronage of the newly founded city. The God of the Sea struck the rock of the Acropolis with his trident, and water as well as a fiery steed sprang forth. Yet the Olympian gods sitting in judgement awarded the coveted prize to the Goddess of Wisdom for her olive tree, symbol of peace and prosperity.

The origin of Athens is lost in the mists of time, in the Neolithic Age, though it is certain that settlers had taken advantage of the opportunities offered by the well protected plain between the mountains and the sea as early as 3000 B.C. Legend credits the Phoenician King Kekrops with the foundation of the town, named after him Kekropia, united with a dozen other villages and rededicated to Athena by his descendant, the Serpent-king Erechtheus, who built the royal palace on the Acropolis. The mythological hero Theseus united the warring small states of Attica under one ruler in the 10th century B.C., but by the early 7th century B.C. monarchy was replaced in most of Greece by the oligarchy of large landowners, and the last king, Kodros, was overthrown by the aristocracy.

History begins with the protracted struggle between these aristocrats and the small farmers for the scarce land. In 621 B.C. the chief magistrate Dracon was entrusted with extraordinary powers to reform justice. These first written laws replaced family vendetta and private vengeance with public trial and punishment, but the provisions concerning mortgages and enslavement for debt were so severe that Draconian has been a byword for extreme harshness ever since. The landless peasants continued to clamour for a redistribution of the large estates, so that in 594 B.C. Solon, one of the Seven Wise Men of antiquity, was appointed to provide a peaceful solution. An aristocrat by birth and merchant by profession, Solon was singularly suited to deal with the pressing social and economic problems, neither as a doctrinaire reformer nor as a reactionary conservative, but according to this famous principle "Nothing in Excess".

His prudent moderation laid the foundation of Athens' greatness, which was further advanced by the tyrant Peisistratus who, together with his son and successor Hippias, dominated the political scene for fifty years. In antiquity tyranny merely meant rule by one man, usually to protect the people from exploitation by the aristocracy, and Peisistratus firmly adhered to Solon's reforms, undertook spectacular public works to reduce unemployment, made Athens a leading cultural centre by attracting philosophers, poets and artists, and transformed the backward city-state he had seized into a commercial power.

Spartan intervention overthrew Hippias' benevolent dictatorship in 510 B.C., so that two years later Cleisthenes was able to promulgate the first truly democratic constitution. Thanks to a series of brilliant statesmen and generals like Themistocles, Cimon and Pericles the free citizens united in the glorious triumphs of the Persian Wars, when the vastly superior numbers of the enemy were defeated at Marathon, Salamis and Plataeae in battles which changed the history of the world.

At thc assumption of power by Pericles in 461 B.C., Athens had become the undisputed leader of Greece, the School of Hellas, and for thirty years was to enjoy the fabulous Golden Age which made it the most beautiful town of antiquity, the fitting home for unsurpassed intellectual and artistic achievements that long outlasted political greatness. The dissaster of the Peloponnesian War (431-404 B.C.) reduced Athens to the status of a secondary power, and despite a short revival under the able leadership of Lycurgus in the fourth century, the ancient, city-states had become an anachronism. The famed orator Demosthenes in vain whipped up some outdated local patriotism by his virulent speeches, but at Chaironia Greek democracy was crushed by the all-conquering Macedonians. Yet Alexander the Great, successive Hellenistic kings and, above all, the Romans were awed by the cultural prestige of Athens, lavished privileges on their proudest procession and rarely interfered in the local government.

For 200 years Athens united an unparallelled galaxy of geniuses in all forms of thought and art; philosophy reached the sublime heights of a Socrates, Plato and Aristotle who have influenced Western reasoning and civilization to this day; poetry blossomed into the superb dramas of Aeschylus, Sophocles and Euripides, Aristophanes transformed gross ribaldry into highly sophisticated political and moral satire; Herodotus' entertaining if inaccurate stories gave way to the admirably objective histories of Thucydides and Xenophon to find a last masterly exponent in Plutarch.

Not that the visual arts lacked behind; Callicrates, Mnesicles and especially Ictinos made the Acropolis into an altar of beauty still breathtaking after 2500 years of neglect, pillage and wanton destruction; Pheidias and Praxiteles chose gold, ivory and marble for their splendid sculptures, inspired by the same wish for perfection which characterized the paintings of Appeles, Polygnotus and Protogenes.

The Roman conquest in 146 B.C. was soon followed by a spiritual conquest-in-reverse, making Athens the cultural capital of the Empire. Young Roman patricians studied there the refinements of the spirit in the philosophical schools and libraries, while large crowds of tourists viewed the unique monuments and art treasures. The second century A.D. witnessed a new flowering, actively supported by the munificence of the Antonine emperors and especially Hadrian, but though imposing by sheer dimensions the public buildings lacked the spontaneous originality of previous ages.

Though St. Paul had preached his famous sermon about the Unknown God in Athens, paganism held sway in the town whose eminence, prosperity and even livelihood depended on profane philosophy. The future Emperor Julian, the Apostate, was steeped in the passing beliefs in the famed schools which were closed by the Emperor Justinian in 529 A.D. This was the deathblow, after the appalling revages of Alaric and his Goths in the preceding century. Repeated depredations by barbaric invaders accentuated the medieval twilight and decay, though even in those dark ages Athenian resilience produced some charming if minute gems of Byzantine architecture in keeping with the sadly diminished state.

The Frankish occupation in 1204 heralded a colourful if incongruous interlude under feudal Burgundian and Florentine dukes, whom Shakespeare introduces somewhat anachronistically into the Midsummer Night's Dream. But picturesque chivalry ended with the Turkish conquest in 1456 which brought misery and ruin, despite Sultan Mohammed II's wholehearted admiration for the ancient monuments which he converted into mosques, adding minarets in a bizarre attempt to adapt classicism for the Moslem faith.

With a single and rather insignificant exception, the nearly four hundred years of Turkish occupation left no positive trace, only everincreasing decay due to the ravages of time, neglect and ignorance. Lightning struck the Propylaea, then used as a powder magazine, which was transferred by Turkish insouciance to the Parthenon, blown up in its turn by a cannon ball fired by Morosini's Venetians in 1687. In the 18th century the sultans granted permission to favoured foreigners to carry away statues and reliefs, of which the Elgin marbles in the British Museum are the best known.

After several destructive sieges during the Greek war of Independence, the Turkish garrison finally surrendered to King Otho in 1833 and the ancient prestige of the poverty-stricken oriental small town of some 6000 inhabitants determined the choise of Athens as capital of the resurrected kingdom.

A group of German architects called by King Otho developed a simple but attractive style of stuccoed façades, ornamental balconies and porches with Ionian columns, which spread round the royal palace long after Otho's abdication, though still bearing his name. Much of it disappeared in the wholesale rebuilding of the 1950's and 1960's, which created a modern town of tall blocks of flats and sprawling suburbs, but most of the public buildings, most of them neo-classical, of the previous century still survive.

Greater Athens, including Piraeus and the suburbs, with close on four million inhabitants has long burst its antique boundaries and extends over more than 150 square miles from the sea to the protective semi-circle of mountains.

# THE ACROPOLIS

Excavations have brought to light traces of pre-Hellenic occupation of the limestone rock rising 230 feet above the surrounding city. A natural fortress, the only accessible approaches from the west were protected by Cyclopean ramparts of huge rough blocks, up to 13 feet thick, in the Mycenaean period.

Erechtheus built the first temple on the reputed site of Athena's contest with Poseidon, to become himself eventually deified and worshipped. From the western battlement below the royal palace King Aegeus flung himself when he saw the black sails of the ship returning from Crete which erroneously proclaimed his son Theseus killed by the Minotaur.

Peisistratus began the transformation of the fortifications into a sanctuary by breaching the tremendous walls with a monumental gate leading to a temple of Artemis, Protectress of the Fortress, and a hundred-foot temple of Athena, all destroyed by the Persians in 480 B.C. This catastrophe provided however, an opportunity to extend the gable-shaped rock by the addition of strong bastions. Themistocles included the broken statues and columns in the revetment and walls, so that the preservation of the unique archaic statues in the Acropolis Museum is due to his haste in refortifying the citadel.

A rare concourse of outstanding architects and sculptors, coupled with the somewhat highhanded use of the Delian League's war chest made it possible for Pericles to create an "Altar to Beauty" on a gigantic scale. Over the space between the magnificent temple were massed superb marble and bronze statues, and high above all rose Athena, Leader in Battle, whose gilded helmet and spear guided the ships to the safe harbour of Piraeus till the Emperor Justinian, in one of the frequent raids on Greek art treasures, shipped Pheidias' colossal statue to Constantinople in the 6th century. Only some marble debris remain from that incomparable forest of sculptures, but the unimpeded view of the Parthenon's honey-coloured soaring columns offers a small compensation for the irreparable loss.

Plundered by Byzantine emperors and barbarian invaders alike the Acropolis served successively as residence for the Orthodox archbishops, the Frankish dukes, who added a medieval tower demolished in 1875, and the Turkish commanders till the extensive destructions in the siege of 1827.

Once the proposal to build a new royal palace into the ruins of the Parthenon had been discarded, King Otho's architects could begin the restoration of the Acropolis, a task which took over a hundred years before it became once more possible to admire the glory that was and is Greece.

*The Acropolis of Athens (restoration)*

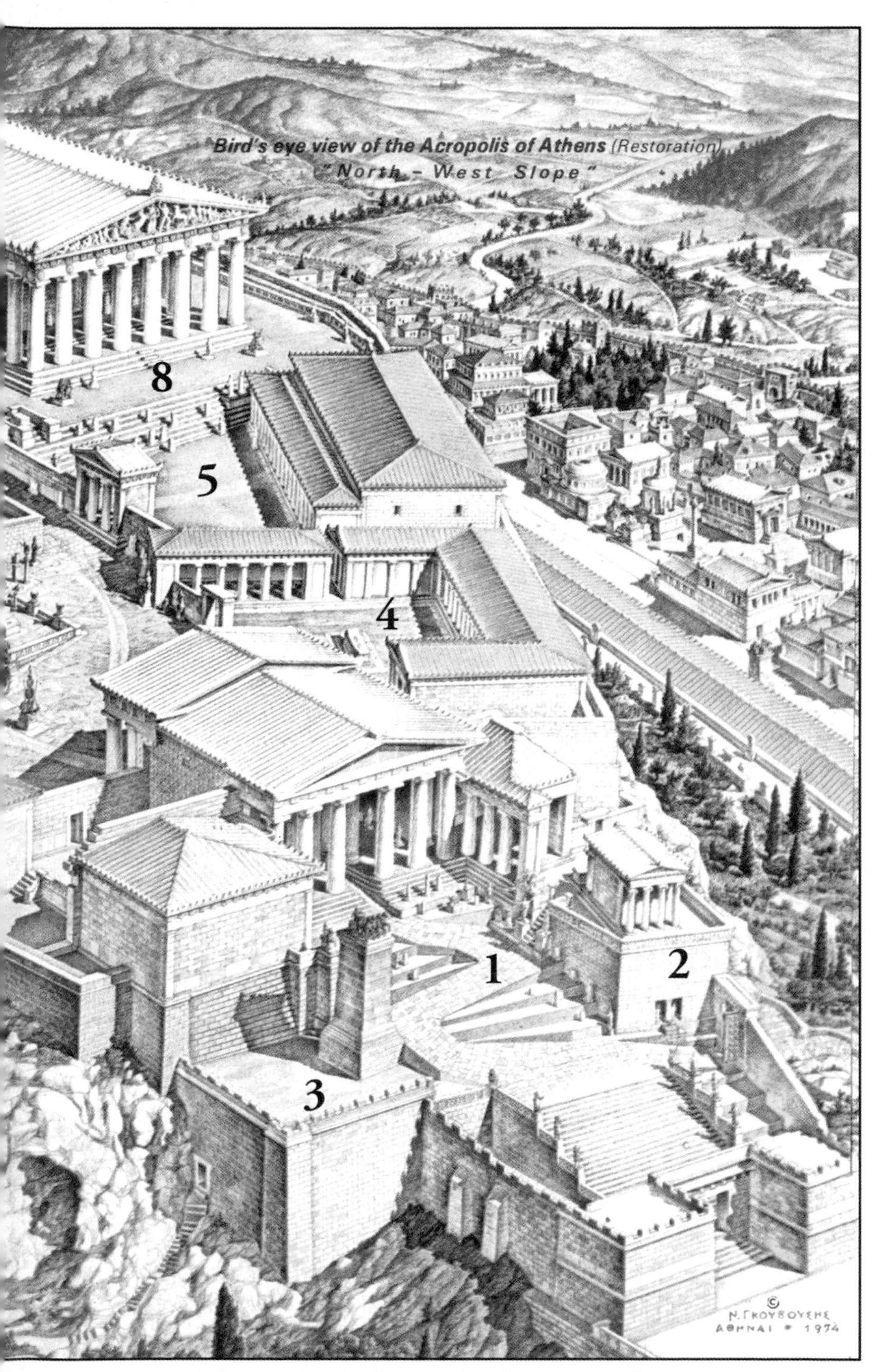


*1. The Propylaea 2. The Temple of Nike 3. Pedestal of Agrippa 4. Vraoneion 5. Chalcothece 6. Bronze statue of Athena 7. Arreforeion 8. Parthenon 9. Erechtheion 10. Temple of Roma*

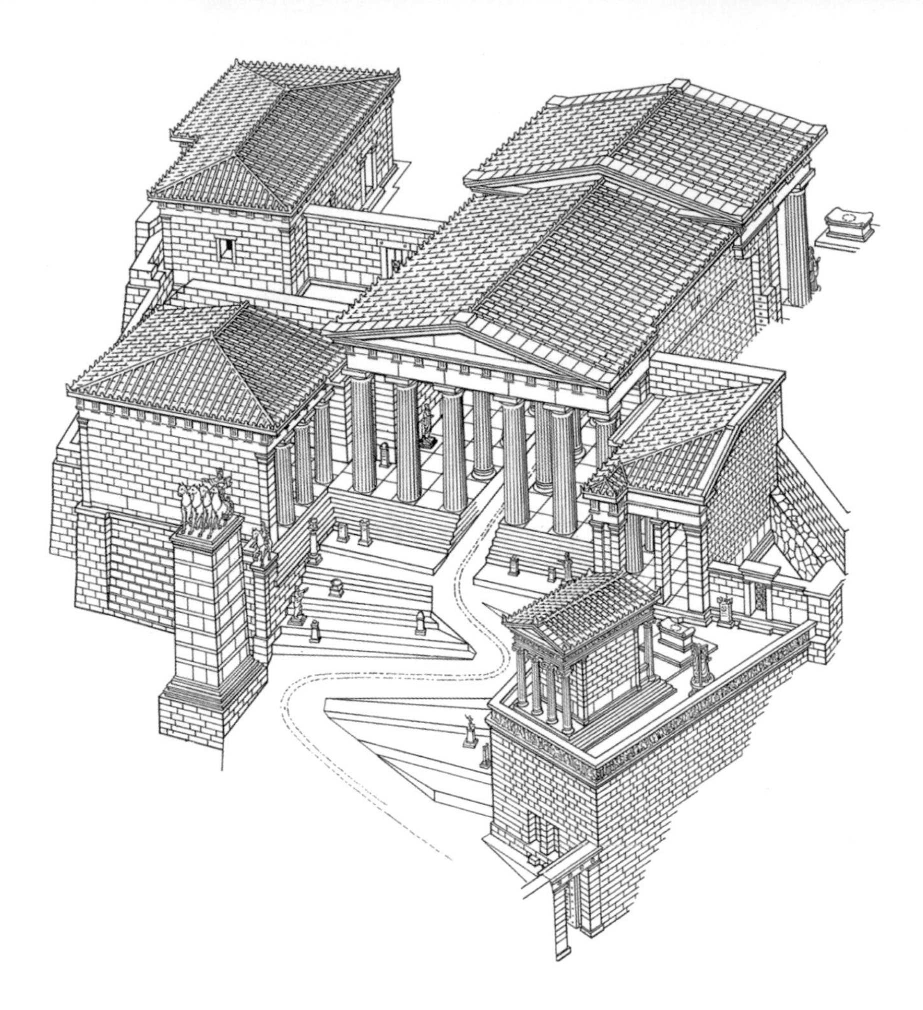

## The Propylaea

Of all the surviving specimens of Athenian art, the Propylaea may be considered the most perfect and most characteristic, a genuine wonder to the whole of Greece.

Leake considers this work as the highest product of the noble architecture of Athens, rivalling the Parthenon itself in its successful execution, and surpassing it in originality and the unique character of its design.

The work of building it was begun during the archonship of Euthumenes in the year B.C. 437. Its architect was

Mnesicles, who finished it in five years. It was reared on the site occupied by an older Propylaea which had been destroyed by the Persians, and which was called the "Nine Gated", from the number probably of its gates. The new building received an inclination towards the S.W., although the older one, as we know from the vestiges of it now existing betwixt the southern side of the Prolylaea and the enclosure of the Acropolis, was turned towards the N.W.

Several authors relate that 2012 talents were expended on the building of this edifice. It was all of Pentelic marble and occupied the western side of the Acropolis, being 170 feet long. This was its composition;

Before it was a flight of steps, 71 feet broad, consisting of about sixteen steps, cut in the middle by the entrance, as it was called, and terminated at its upper end by the largest gate of the Propylaea, through which the horses, the wagons, and the sacred chariot entered to the Acropolis during the Panathenaic festival. This large gate divided the whole building into two colonnades or stoas, each consisting of six fluted columns of the Doric order, on the top of which was the pediment. These columns were 5 feet in diameter and 29 feet in height. On either side of this large central gate there were other smaller gates through which pedestrians ascended to the Acropolis.

Of the stoas, the western one, 43 feet in depth, was turned towards the town. The eastern one, half as high again, from the nature of the ground, looked towards the Acropolis. It was called Propylaea because it stood before the above mentioned gates (πύλαι). Each of these stoas had three Doric columns in front. The central chamber or portico behind the hexastyle stoa was 60 feet broad, 44 feet deep, and 39 feet high. It was covered by a roof with marble lacunaria, and richly decorated with gold. The roof was supported on the inner side by two rows of three Ionic columns each, which columns with the two central Doric ones, adorned the outer stoa.

The eastern side of this chamber was built on solid plinths of dark Eleusinian stone. The union of the two styles gives so much harmony and symmetry to the building, that it is mentioned with astonishment, not only by the Athenians, but also by their enemies.

The Propylaea consisted of a centre, but it had something like wings projecting on either side. Of these three divisions the chief one is the true Propylaea, or ornamental approach to the five gates leading to the Acropolis. The row of columns on the right was adorned with the Temple of the Wingless Victory; the wing on the opposite side enclosed a building, inside of which were the splendid paintings of Polygnotus and Timenaetus which time had already begun to destroy in Pausanias' day. The roof, richly sculptured and finely adorned, was supported on marble beams, which rested on the walls and on the architraves of the two rows of Ionic columns. There were three layers of such beams the whole length of the Propylaea.

These beams, which covered the side wings, were 22 feet in length, and those of the central part were 17 feet, with corresponding breadth and length.

Such masses of stonc projccting on thc roof of such a building supported the painted and variously ornamented roof, which justly excited a man so sparing in his praises as Pausanias to refer to them with the greatest admiration. The southern wing of the Propylaea, or right wing as we ascend to the Acropolis, consists of a stoa without an edifice, 26 feet long and 17 feet broad. Towards the western side of this wing stands the little Temple of Wingless Victory, and in this was the statue of Hecate, the Epipyrgidia. From this point the sea is visible, and here it was that Aegeus threw himself down and died, according to tradition, when the black-sailed ship that carried the children to Crete was returning.

A good deal of the Propylaea is still preserved; there are now twenty-four columns, of which thirteen are in good condition.

Whilst the Propylaea was being built, the most industrious of the workmen fell from the roof, and was in danger of death. Pericles was in great perplexity, when Athena appeared to him in a dream and taught him how the man might be cured. Pericles followed her advice, and the result being satisfactory, he at once erected a bronze statue to Athena Hygieia, close to the spot where an altar to the same goddess was built at a later period by Pyrrhus, the circular base of which may still be seen on the left of the Acropolis as we enter through the Propylaea, resting against the wall.

When the Franks ruled in Athens, they transformed the northern wing, of Pinacotheca, into their official court, and on the sourthern wing they erected the tower, which has been levelled to the ground by Dr. Schliemann. The common people called the Propylaea, the "Palace of Themistocles", and afterwards the "Armoury of Lycurgus". In the year 1455, when the Turks were lords of Athens, they changed the buildings into a storehouse of arms and a gunpowder magazine. But when these were struck by lightning in 1656, just at the moment, it is said, when the Turkish commander was preparing to cannonade the Christians assembled about St. Demetrius, an explosion ensued which destroyed the entablature of the eastern stoa. That on the western side remained intact not only until 1656, when it was seen by Spon and Wheler, but even until 1687, when the engineer Bernadas sketched it after Morozini's siege.

When Athens became free, the Propylaea came into her possession without a roof. But when once the surrounding soil was excavated and cleared of its later walls, as much as possible of its ancient form was restored to it.

## The Temple of Wingless Victory

On the southern brow of the Acropolis hill, to the right as we ascend to the Propylaea, stands the small, but very graceful Temple of Wingless Victory. This temple is of Pentelic marble and of the Ionic order; it now stands on its original site, and is all but perfect. It is perched on a tower-like eminence which was of old called a tower; and the statue of the Three-shaped Hecate of Alcamenes which stood in it was called the Epipurgidias. This tower (or pyrgos) on which the temple stands, consists of a wall of light marble (πώρινος), built in equal courses. But towards the top, on its N. and W. side, the marble pavement terminates in a little projection, thus forming a tiny cornice. All the upper surface of the tower stands at the same level is the foundation of the Propylaea.

This temple stands upon a base 3 feet high, and is 27 feet long from E. to W., and 18 feet broad. The height of the columns, including their bases and capitals, in 13 feet, their diameter at the base is 0'52 m., and at the top 0'43 m. The whole height of the temple from the base to the summit of the pediment is 23 feet.

This temple is amphiprostyle and tetrastyle, having four columns at its two smaller sides, i.e., at the E. and W.; these constitute its two porticoes. It consists of a single simple cella, enclosing within it the statue, and looking towards the E. It was open about the pronaos, and the roof was supported by two pilasters instead of by a wall. On the lacunaria of the stoas, chiefly towards the western side, we may still see traces of colouring; their columns have this peculiarity, that they are very slender monoliths, having twenty-four flutings. Their base is very narrow and deep, the upper part being ornamented with horizontal flutings. The capital was without a hypotrachelium. The whole temple was encircled on the exterior by a frieze 1 foot 4 inches high, adorned with an unbroken line of pictures in high relief.

This frieze, when seen by Spon and Wheler, represented an assembly of gods and ideal groups, a fight of Greeks with Greeks and with Persians, and as some suppose, that of Cimon in Eurymedon, where Greek Cypriotes fought as Persian allies; or according to others, the battle of the Athenians with the Thebans and Euboeans, or that of Marathon, or rather that of Plataea. The four fragments in the British Museum are easily distinguished by the crescentshaped shields and wide vestments of the Persians, and by the great circular shields and the helmets of the Greeks, as also from the latter being either nude or clad in a short chiton.

On the other side, a sitting form, as of a deity, appears in the centre, and around it are many other forms, probably those of gods; it is difficult to say what the remainder represented, as they are almost completely rubbed away. It was originally composed of fourteen pieces of stone, of which twelve, or fragments of twelve, now exist, some of them being frightfully mutilated and difficult to describe. Parts of the frieze were carried away to England by Lord Elgin, and in places are clay mouldings filling up the holes in the zone. A portion which was found here has been restored to its old place.

We cannot define accurately the time when this temple was built. No author mentions it, but from the bas-reliefs themselves we may conclude that it was built after the Persian war, probably under Cimon, in recollection of splendid victories won against the barbarians, and in honour of the goddess Nike, or Victory. It was called Wingless, like the statue or ancient image, because the Athenians themselves had given it this name, supposing that it would stay in their town and would never leave them. Nike was imaged as Wingless, and identified with Athena; she was like a young girl holding in her right hand the fruit of the pomegranate, a symbol of warlike valour.

On the sides of the antae of this temple there may be seen some regular holes, which make it evident that these portions were protected by railings.

This temple was preserved till 1679, when Spon and Wheler visited Athens. But in 1751 no part of it was to be seen except a few remains and fragments lying prostrate.

The excavations carried out by the Archaeological Society in 1835, under the superintendence of the German archaeologists Ross and Schaubert, resulted in the discovery of many stones, and out of these the temple has been rebuilt. Set up and repaired as much as was possible, it is presented to us to-day almost as it was in its first and perfect state.

## The Parthenon

The Parthenon may be considered the most perfect and the most magnificent ruin in the world, although a whole museum was carried away to England by Lord Elgin from the spoils of this one temple.

This temple of the Virgin Athena, the Goddess of Wisdom, was erected by the illustrious son of Xanthippos, the Olympian Pericles, by the skill of the architects Ictinus, Callicrates, and Carpion, under the supervision of Phidias. It was built on the ruins and foundations of a more ancient temple, which may still be plainly seen, because the later one was three or four metres larger, by a visible addition, and was all built of the white marble of Mount Pentelicus, except the tiles of the roof, which were of Parian marble. Situated on the highest platform of the Acropolis, the Parthenon rose so high above the western approach that the pavement of its peristyle was on the same level as the capitals of the eastern colonnade (stoa) of the Propylaea. It was called the Hecatompedon on account of its beauty, as we are told by Harpocration. The work of building was completed B.C. 438. We do not know when it was begun, but we do know that that of the Propylaea lasted five years, and it is thus possible that that of the Parthenon occupied a longer period. Leake conjectures that 1000 talents or 6,000,000 drachmas of that period were spent upon it.

The temple forms a long tetragon, of which the shorter sides are the façades. Its principal front was turned to the E., in contrast with all other ancient Doric temples, in order, as Vitruvius says, that the statue of the goddess might appear as if hovering over the city at the dawn of day.

It is truly painful to reflect that only two centuries ago this famous temple was still in all its grandeur, as well preserved as is the Theseum.

It had survived through times of war and insurrection, and through revolutions in religion, for more than 2000 years, and none of its external beauties had been destroyed. The sculptures of its pediments were still in their places and had been very little injured. The metopes were also there, and the architrave was perfect in all its parts, except that of the pronaos, which had been stripped away along with the columns of the eastern pronaos for the purpose of making room for a Christian apse. In the outer part no injury whatever had occurred, and we might, therefore, at that period, have admired the most perfect work of Greek architecture in its every detail.

In this state it was preserved until the year 1687, when a bomb from the batteries of Morozini was suddenly thrown into the gunpowder magazine which the Turks had inside the temple; thus rendering it the heap of ruins it is. All the eastern side was overthrown; of the southern side only a mutilated and irrecognisable head of one of the Sun's horses was saved.

The western frieze is to-day preserved amidst the foggy atmosphere of London, one of the statues was carried away by the Venetians, and the remains of the two others may still be perceived at the end of this frieze. But it is nevertheless uncertain if the catastrophe of 1687 was as destructive to the inner portion as to the outer one.

This temple had been turned into a Christian church many centuries earlier, and consequently great internal changes had taken place that it might be transformed according to Christian ideas, and not a few changes had likewise been made on the exterior. We do not know when this occurred, but probably in the very earliest years of Christianity the master-pieces of classical art quite lost their glitter. Had the insanity of the Iconoclasts prevailed, the idolatrous sculptures which still remain to us would never have been found so uninjured as they were at the beginning of the last century, because by the mere transformation of the temple into a Christian church very few changes, indeed only the unavoidable ones, were made. In the first place they removed the chief entrance from the eastern to the western façade (or opisthodomos), which, on account of its position with regard to the Propylaea, was naturally destined to be so used. A second change was the transformation of the opisthodomos or posticum, into the pronaos or vestibule of the church, a change which was quite indispensable. The treasury was,

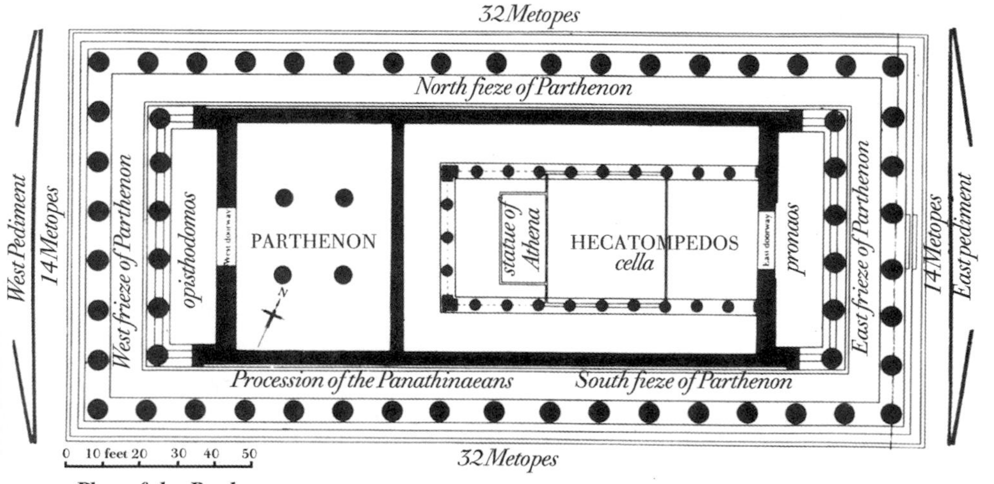


Plan of the Parthenon

in ancient times, a necessary adjunct, and therefore about a third of the temple space was partitioned off; but the Christians made a better use of the area and opened up all the interior. They accomplished the change by making a central passage leading to the door through the wall of the cella, thus uniting the two parts of the temple, the two side walls being preserved. At length the greatest change occurred by their closing the ancient eastern entrance, and erecting a portico inside of it, of which the traces still exist.

The length of the temple is 228 feet, the breadth 101 feet, and the height as far as the top of the pediment 66 feet. It consists of a cella surrounded by eight columns on either front, and seventeen on either side (counting the corner columns twice). It was thus surrounded by forty-six columns. The diameter of these columns was at the base 6 feet 1½ inch, and the height 34 feet.

This simple peristyle surrounds the building, and with the walls of the temple forms a graceful colonnade. A second row of pillars behind the first stood upon bases, and was continued to each façade, leaving between itself and the wall of the building a free space, that on the eastern façade being called a pronaos, or vestibule, that on the façade towards the Piraeus being called opisthodomos. Both the pronaos and the opisthodomos contained the public treasure, and were shut off by railings fastened into the columns, the holes being visible to this day. The area of the temple was divided into two unequal parts by a perpendicular wall having a door of communication. The larger of these two parts was called the cella and was 90 feet in length, the western portion or opisthodomos was about 43 feet.

The cella was the chief temple, in which stood the gold and ivory statue of Athena made by Phidias, 26 cubits, or about 40 feet high. The naked parts of the statue were of ivory, the dress and ornaments of gold; the goddess was

*The statue of Athena Parthenos inside the Parthenon (Restoration)*

represented as standing clad in a chiton or robe down to the feet, and holding in her right hand a spear, an image of Victory was in her left; she was girded with the aegis, a Gorgon's head in its centre; on her head was a helmet; the shield lay by her left side; a little behind was a serpent, and on the pedestal was wrought the birth of Pandora. According to Thucydides, the whole weight of the gold was 40 talents, according to Philochorus 44, and according to others, 50. Lachares stripped off this gold. Opinions are divided about the site of this statue.

The roof of the two above - mentioned apartments was upheld by internal rows of columns; in the eastern apartment were twenty-three Doric ones, supporting two roofs, one situated above the other, ten columns being on each side, but three only on the western side. The diameter of these columns at the base was about 3½ feet. Of the walls which formed the temple nothing now remains except those of the opisthodomos, and these are partly dilapidated. The walls of the cella have disappeared, and their ruins are scattered round the place. The pillars which form the inner peristyle of the cella are no longer preserved, we know only that they were of the Doric order.

The temple is raised three layers above the grounds. These layers now form three steps, betwixt which appear the traces of three smaller steps. The temples of the ancients, when dedicated to a god, had always an odd number of steps, in order, as Vitruvius points out, that a man who approached one of them would place his right foot on the first step, and would afterwards enter the chief temple or cella with the same foot.

## THE METOPES OF THE PARTHENON

The external dispositions of every temple had almost always some relation to the deity who was worshipped in it. Thus the types on the exterior of the Parthenon were closely bound up with the history and mythology of the goddess Athena, and recall the ceremonies performed in her honour.

In the first place, the pediments of the gables were filled by two sculptural compositions, each of which was about 80 feet long, and by twenty-four statues of almost colossal size. The eastern, or principal front, represented the Birth of Athena from the head of Zeus; the western one, the quarrel of the same goddess with Poseidon about the soil of Attica.

There were ninety-two metopes, of which fourteen are preserved in two façades of the building. Fifteen were carried away by Lord Elgin, who, by way of compensation, built the great clock which now stands in the market-place. One is in the museum in Paris, and two are preserved on the Acropolis. Of the remainder not a trace is to be found. It is well known that these were lost off Cape Malea, when Lord Elgin's ship was sunk, along with most of the other ornaments of the frieze. The whole portion of the frieze which was not destroyed by the bombs of the Venetian Morozini is preserved in the British Museum.

On the frieze was a representation of the Panathenaic festival, which was held every four years; and about the centre of the eastern front were twelve deities; on the northern front was the battle between the Amazons and Athena; and upon the southern one the deeds of the Athenians, of various heroes, and the Battle of the Centaurs. The frieze of the temple, the row of metopes, and the two pediments, were adorned with wonderfully sculptured ornaments, the different parts of the entablature, the conduit for rain-water, the cymatia of the mural architrave, and the capitals of the columns, were all variously embellished with painted maeanders and leaf-work designs (ανθέμια) in keeping with the many-coloured robes and other adjuncts of the statues.

*A view of Athens from the east in Hadrians time (restoration)*

The shields from the battle of Granicus, sent by Alexander the Great, were hung from the architrave on the eastern side. Near them was the following ambitious inscription, in bronze letters, "Alexander, son of Philip, and the Greeks, all except the Lacedaemonians, from the barbarians of Asia". The traces of the shields, as if sketched by the sun, may be seen to this day. We can see also the holes into which the letters were nailed. The inner walls of the cella were adorned with writings. Those of the vestibule were partly painted by Protogenes of Caunos, and in the Hecatompedon there were prictures representing Themistocles and Heliodorus.

• The Panathenaea was the greatest and most impressive of the Athenian festivals. It was celebrated in honour of Athena Polias, a title which the goddess bore as protectress of the city. The word Panathenaea means the festival observed in common by all the tribes of Attica. There were two kinds of Panathenaeae, the lesser and the greater. The former was celebrated every year, the latter every four years. It lasted for twelve days, that is, from the seventeenth to the twenty-eighth day of the month Hecatombaeon (July).

In this festival the peplum of Athena was carried to her temple in a magnificent procession; games were held; there were costly sacrifices of oxen, foot races, horse races, musical and gymnastic contests, torch races, and minstrels who sang the Homeric poems. The peplum was not carried to the temple by men, but was suspended from the mast of a ship. The ship itself was formerly kept near the Areopagus (Paus. A. 29,1). Afterwards it was drawn along the ground by a subterranean contrivance.

The procession started from the Ceramicus, close to the Leocorium (Thucydides, A. 20). It proceeded towards the temple of Demeter (the Eleusinium), and thence by the Pelasgic wall to the temple of the Pythian Apollo on the Pnyx, and from thence to the Acropolis, where the statue of Athena was covered with the peplum. The whole population of Attica took part in this Panathenaic procession, some on foot, some on horseback, and some in chariots. This we see from the friezes of the cella of the Parthenon.

The daughters of the first families in Athens carried baskets on their heads, containing offerings to the goddess, and from this they were named "κανηφόροι". As for the Metoekoe, or resident foreigners, the men carried trays at this festival, their wives pitchers, and their daughters sunshades. This law was enacted in order to distinguish them from Athenian citizens. Prisoners were set free throughout all the days that the Great Panathenaea lasted. (Demosthenes, Falsa Legatio, 394)

## The Erechtheum

The Erechtheum, the most sacred and mythical of all the temples in Athens, consists of three portions.

First, of the Temple of Athena Polias, which had its portico towards the east, and occupies a space about as large as that of half the whole temple.

Second, of the Temple of Erechtheus.

Third, of the Temple of the Nymph of Maiden Pandrosus, one of the daughters of Cecrops.

These three portions together constitute a whole which is difficult either to describe or to interpret, albeit much has been written about it. This temple was the most ancient sanctuary on the Acropolis. It was usually called the Erechtheum, as we are told by Pausanias.

Amongst the inscriptions of the 92nd Olympiad which treat about the erection of this edifice, it is not called a temple, but a house, as having been built by Erechtheus, who was buried in it; and therefore the part of the temple where his tomb was, was called the Erechtheum proper.

This Erechtheus is represented by Homer as having

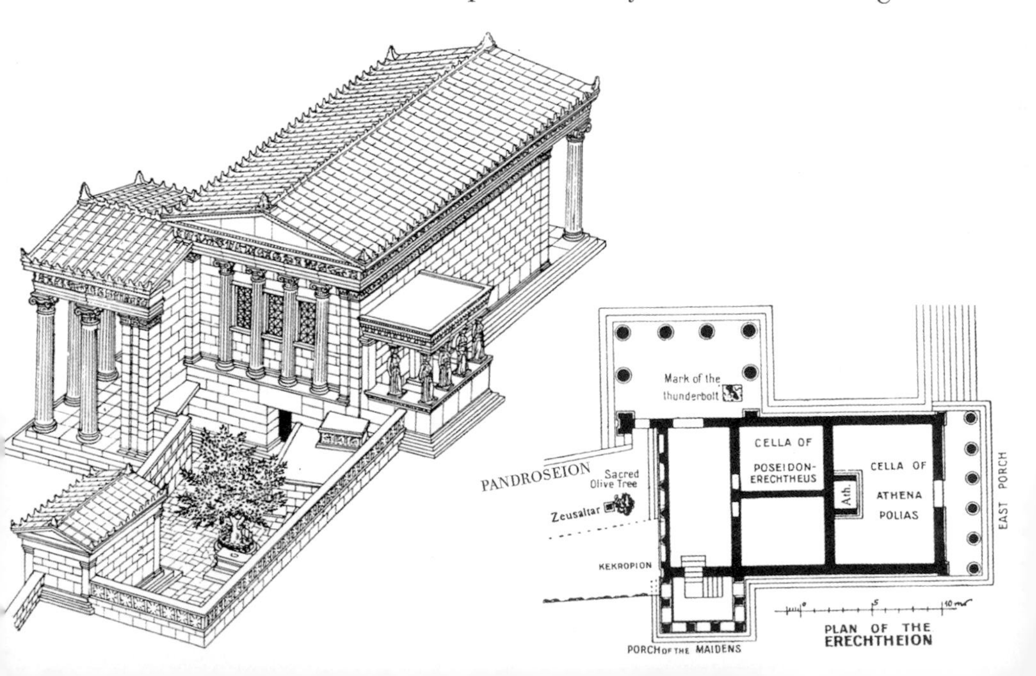

been a child of the earth, and having been reared by the goddess Athena, who, having received him, shut him up in a bag, and gave him into the custody of the sisters Agraulos, Pandrosus, and Herse, daughters of Cecrops. Agraulos and Herse, moved by curiosity, opened the bag. Seeing the child in the form of a serpent they at once went mad, and threw themselves down from the steepest part of the Acropolis. But as Pandrosus had obeyed the behest of the goddess, a part of the temple named the Pandroseum was dedicated to her; and there she received appropriate honours. Agraulos was buried at the foot of the Acropolis. Erechtheus was worshipped in the Erechtheum under the name of Poseidon Erechtheus, as being a son of Poseidon; and one of the family of the Butades, who traced their descent to him, was the hereditary priest of the temple.

Erechtheus was considered to have been the founder of the temple, inasmuch as the worship of Athena was chiefly established by him. But we know from Homer that a Temple of Athena existed on the Acropolis before the birth of Erechtheus. In the colonnade of the temple there were altars to Poseidon, Erechtheus, Butos and Hephaestus. In the temple, probably on the western wall, was the most ancient statue of Athena Polias, protectress of the city. The statue was made of olive-wood, and was said to have fallen from heaven. It was called "Palaeon", as being the most ancient of all.

Here was also the sacred olive-tree which Athena caused to sprout from her spear in the quarrel with Poseidon, and which flourished in the temple without ever increasing in size, being therefore called the "Quite crooked". But when this temple was burnt by the Persians, the holy tree remained unhurt, or rather when burnt, sprouted anew on the following day to the length of a cubit. On the foundation of the burnt temple a new one was built, just as the Parthenon had been; but this temple too was burnt.

There was also here a well of salt water called "the

Erechtheian Sea", or simply "the sea". It was produced by Poseidon when he struck the rock with his trident, and left the impression on it, whose traces are to-day to be seen. It was thought that the plashing of the sea could be heard here whenever the south wind blew. In front of this was the inextinguishable golden lamp, which was dedicated to the goddess by Callimachus, and which burned night and day. It was filled with oil only once a year, and burnt by a wick of fine flaxen threads, for which reason it was called the "ἄσβεστος λύχνος". Its smoke was drawn up as far as the roof by a brazen palm-tree suspended over it.

It is mentioned that the grave of Cecrops was also here.

The whole building was in the Ionic style, and forms a striking contrast to the Doric style of the Parthenon. The shape of the Erechtheum differs from that of every other Greek temple. Greek temples were always long, with two colonnades, one at the east and one at the west side. The Erechtheum, nevertheless, though it was long and had a colonnade on the eastern front, had no corresponding one at the opposite end. But a wing projected from either portion towards the N. and S., cutting the temple crosswise. The temple consequently has three stoas, which may be distinguished as the eastern, the northern, and the southern porticoes.

The anomalous form of the temple arises partly from the unevenness of the ground. The eastern portico stands on a floor about 8 feet higher than the northern one; but the spirit of the Athenian architects triumphed over these difficulties. It consists of six Ionic columns standing before the wall of the cella, the ends of which are cut, and terminate in pilasters opposite to the end of the columns. Five of these columns still stand in situ.

The northern portico was in front of the other chief entrance. It likewise consisted of six Ionic columns, but only four of these are to the front. The other two stand one of either side. Far within the entrance was opened the splendid gate from the Pandroseum, betwixt the two doors. All these columns now stand in situ. They are 3½ feet higher, and ½foot thicker than those of the eastern portico. Before these porticoes were the two great doors of which we have spoken. They were very richly adorned. Before each stood an altar of incense.

The southern portico was entirely different. Instead of columns, six wonderful statues of virgins stood, dressed in their Panathenaic costumes, carrying easily and unconstrainedly on their heads the light entablature, consisting of six Ionic architraves with rosettes and ornaments, and above these a cymatium with thick little Ionic dentils without a frieze. There are four on the façade, and one on each of the sides, so as to form a hexastyle and prostyle temple. Of these maidens, five out of the six are preserved, the sixth, on the northern portico, was pillaged by Lord Elgin. A copy* in gypsum replaces it. It stands upon a foundation 8 feet above the outer surface. The roof is level, and is 15 feet above the floor of the building. We are unable to say anything, either about the doorway, or about the eastern wall, but we observe that at the antae of the long walls on the northern and southern sides, there exist, towards the interior, smaller pilasters opposite to them, and that this looks like the beginning of a wall, which nevertheless probably never existed. Yet there were railings.

A similar portico is found on the western side, corresponding to the one of which we have spoken, but since in it the surface of the ground is quite 10 feet lower, the architect was obliged to raise a wall till he came to about the line of the eastern side. On account of this elevation it was naturally impossible to have a portico in this portion, but there was a kind of portico of four Ionic engaged columns corresponding to the four columns of the eastern

* Athenian tradition says that when this one maiden was stolen, the others moaned the whole night for their departed sister.

side. Within the temple we find a side similar to the wall in the portico. The other minor distinctions of the temple are very difficult to describe, and can only be understood by means of a sketch.

In the temple of Athena Poliuchos was likewise the guardian or Erichthonian serpent, the sacred symbol of Athena, whose dwelling in the Erechtheum was called the drakaulos. There honey-cakes were placed every month. The position of this drakaulos cannot now be accurately defined.

Within this enclosure were several statues, referred to by Pausanias, such as the colossal bronze ones of Erechtheus.

The extant building of the Erechtheum is not the one mentioned by Homer in the Odyssey, nor was it another building earlier than the time of the Medes. The situation alone is the same as that of the older temple erected by the Athenians after the Persian war. Nevertheless we do not know exactly when it was built. We learn, however, from an inscription during the archonship of Diocles, B.C. 409, that the work was then not quite finished; as Xenophon relates in his "Hellenica" during the archonship of Callias, B.C. 401, the ancient temple of Athena was burnt, but since it was a stone one, as the record of the inscription testifies, we conjecture that many of the stone portions of that temple remained unhurt, and were of service for the temple built about B.C. 406. But the fact of the temple having been built between B.C. 406 and B.C. 393 is only a supposition arising from a passage in Xenophon, which states that this temple was not finished before B.C. 393, because the Athenians under Cimon had not yet raised their long walls and could not then occupy themselves with the building of this temple.

The architects were Philocles of Acharnae and Archilochus of Agrylla, as we learn from some inscriptions. The most important parts of the building which are now preserved were their work.

The Parthenon was the most magnificent, and the Erechtheum the most graceful building which ancient art ever produced when at its highest point of development. Both are equally astonishing, whether we regard them as a whole or in their most minute details.

The bases of its Ionic columns are adorned with very rich and accurately executed plaited work. The leaf-work patterns on the neck, on the capitals, and on the plinths of the walls are incomparable specimens of ornamental sculpture, on account of their grace, their richness, and their beauty. The volutes of the capitals were ornamented, as we learn from inscriptions, with gilded bronze-work about the eyes, and with stones of many colours, some of which are preserved. The inner volutes were coloured in encaustic with meanders, the Iacunaria with stars. Those on the northern side and those of the caryatides had applied stars for gilded bronze, which is manifest from the holes destined for the reception of the nails which fastened them. The frieze was in keeping with the grace of its surroundings. It consisted of small white statues fastened on to black Eleusinian stone, and made an impression of the greatest beauty from the union of the two colours. We are informed by the same inscriptions that the temple had a roof, which was almost certainly of wood since not a trace of a stone one now appears. It was lighted by six holes or skylights. It is worthy of remark that, as we are informed by the inscriptions found there, the architects of this inimitable temple received a pay of one drachma per diem.

The Erechtheum is an exception to all other Athenian monuments, as having corbels beneath the cornice, like all the other temples in Attica, excepting those of Athens.

---

*Aerial view of the Acropolis with Mt. Lycavitos in the background*

*Aerial view of the Acropolis from the North-West*

*he Acropolis seen from the hill of Philopappus*

*Acropolis view from Lycabettus hill*

*The Acropolis seen from the hill of Pnyx*

*The Propylaea of the Acropolis*

*The Propylaea of the Acropolis*

*The Propylaea's eastern inner colonnade*

*The Temple of Wingless Victory (Nike)*

*The Parthenon from the Propylaea*

*The Parthenon*

## DECORATION OF THE PARTHENON

The architectural magnificence provided the fitting shell for Pheidias' ornaments. The brightly coloured exterior sculptural decorations were of splendid craftsmanship - 44 figures in the pediments. In the East, the birth of Athena emerging fully armed from the head of Zeus; in the West, the contest of Athena and Poseidon. 92 metopes depicted the battles of the giants, the Lapiths and Centaurs. The crowning glory was the second frieze of continuous bas-reliefs extending for 524 feet to encompass all the participants in the Panathenaean procession. What escaped destruction is now mostly in the British Museum.

*The West Pediment of the Parthenon and the western part of the famous frieze*

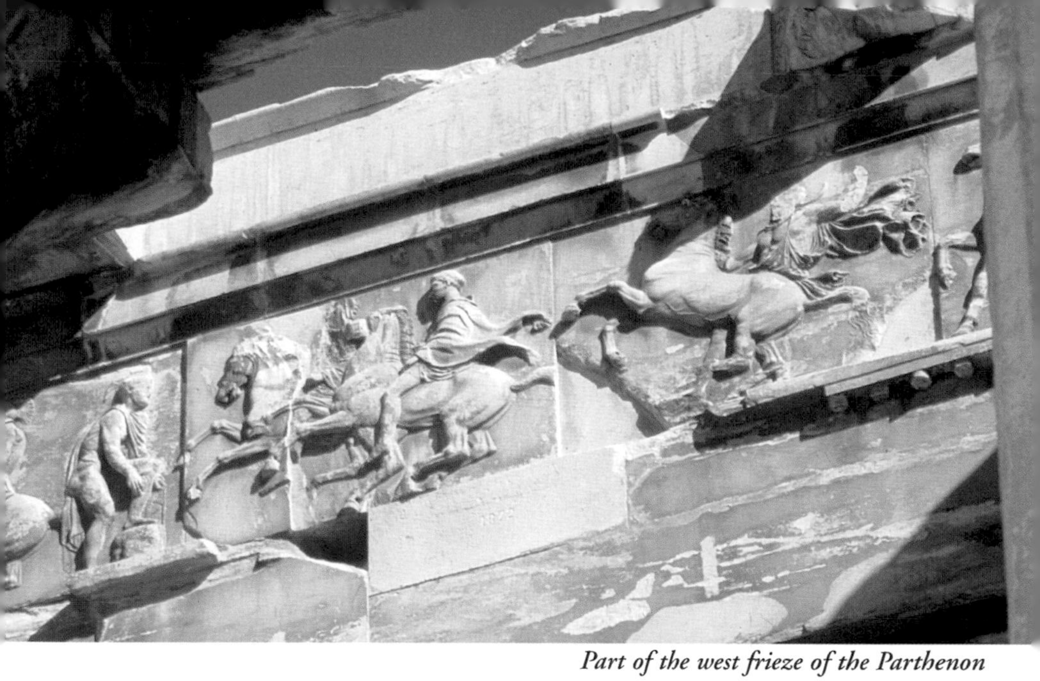

*Part of the west frieze of the Parthenon*

*Part of the east pediment of the Parthenon*

*Erechtheion From south-east*

*The porch of the famous Caryatides on the Erechtheion—*

*Erechtheion From west*

## THE ACROPOLIS MUSEUM

This museum contains an unrivalled collection of archaic sculptures, miraculously preserved in the hasty refortification after the destruction by the Persians in 480 B.C.

In room I are two pediments, of Treasuries, the one representing Hercules killing the Lernaean Hydra. The gorgon head and the Lioness rending a Bull belong to the beginning of the 6th century B.C.

Room II displays the pediment of "Peisistratus" temple of Athena, and the superb Calf-bearer, a youth carrying a calf slung across his shoulders, one of the finest archaic statues.

Rooms III, IV and V are highlighted by a large kouros (youth), a horseman, a hunting dog, but above all the unique korai (maidens) representing either Athena's high priestesses or supplicants, in a standardised version of a young woman, her enigmatic smile contemptuous under the elaborate headdress. The postures, however, illustrate the gradual liberation from archaic rigidity of body, arms and legs at the beginning of the 6th century B.C. to the more natural extended hand of the middle period, and the rich folds of the Ionian tunic accentuating the lines of the body at the dawn of classicism.

Rooms VI to IX are dominated by classical sculptures; a splendid bas-relief of Athena leaning on her lance, a superb horse, youths and korai, and fragments from the frieze of the Parthenon, Pheidias' wonderful representation of the Panathenaean procession, with its unsurpassed naturalness of men and beast moving and at rest. The Frieze of Victories, a gift of Alcibiades that once decorated the parapet surrounding the temple of Athena Nike, must have been likewise of exceptional workmanship, judging from the bas-relief of Nike unfastening her Sandal.

Hellenistic and Roman finds are in room IX, while the plastermodels of the Parthenon's pediments in room VII give a useful idea of the sculptures' full glory.

*Acropolis museum:*
*The "Moschophoros" (Galf-bearer)*

*Acropolis museum:*
*Statue of an archaic Kore*

*Acropolis museum: Nike (Victory) loosening her sandal*

*Acropolis museum: Horsemen. Slab from the North Side of the Parthenon frieze*

*Gods: Poseidon, Apollo, Artemis, Slab from the East Side of the Parthenon frieze*

*Theatre of Dionysus. (Restoration)*

## THE THEATRE OF DIONYSUS

With the opening of the huge Theatre of Dionysus by Peisistratus in 534 B.C. a new art form was born. Above the comfortable high-backed front seats reserved for the literary jury and the throne of Dionysus' high priest, 13,000 citizens crowded the 67 tiers during the Dionysia spring festivals to listen to the immortal works of Aeschylus, Sophocles, Euripides and Aristophanes, three tragic and five comic poets each year.

The circular stage and the sculptured frieze, depicting the progress of the wine god, are Roman, as also the marble railing put up when the theatre was converted for gladiatorial spectacles. The cost of production was defrayed by wealthy citizens who commemorated the prizewinning play with choragic monuments, two of which still stand above the theatre.

The foundations of Pericles' Odeon, believed to be the most beautiful concert hall, lie to the east.

*The Theatre of Dionysus*

*Reliefs from the proscenion of Dionysus theatre*

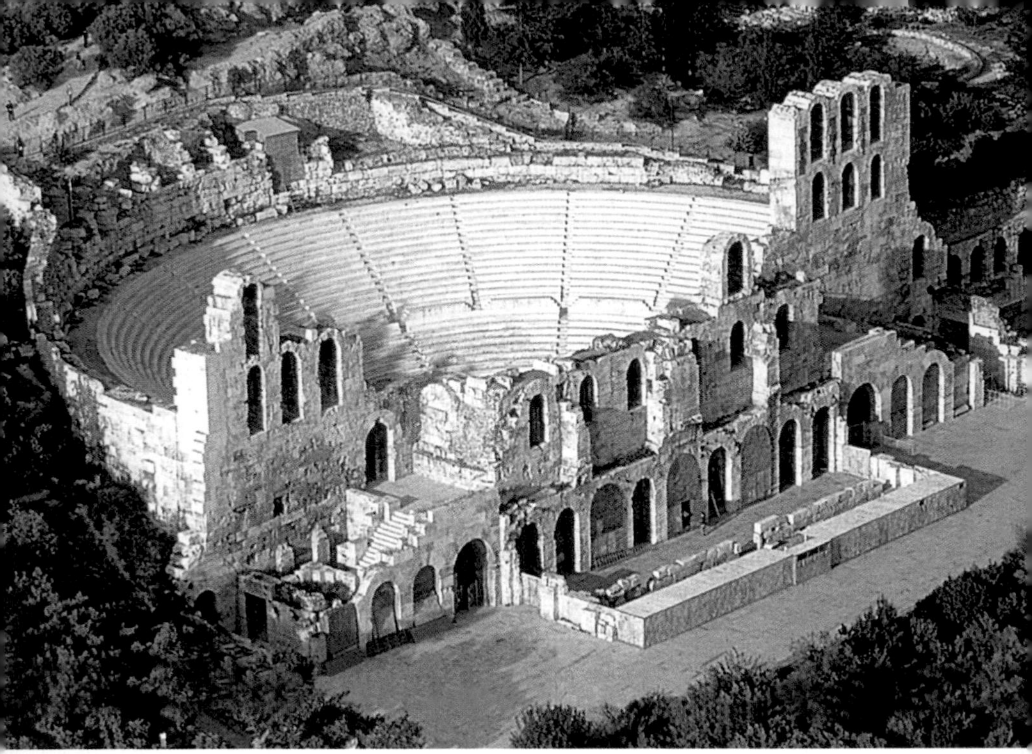
*The Odeon of Herodes Atticus*

*The Odeon of Herodes Atticus below the floodlit Acropolis*

*The Odeon of Herodes Atticus*

## THE ODEON OF HERODES ATTICUS

The southern slope of the Acropolis is mainly dedicated to the dramatic arts. Herodes Atticus, the immensely wealthy banker and friend of the Emperor Hadrian, had the 5000-seat Odeon carved into the rock in 161 A.D. as memorial to his wife Regilla. Expertly restored, it provides a superb setting for the annual Summer Festival of Music and Drama.

The adjoining 179-yard-long colonnade was the gift of an earlier benefactor, King Eumenes II of Pergamon. Originally intended as a covered walk for philosophers, it was later connected to the Odeon and used as a foyer.

*The Areopagus*

## THE AREOPAGUS

On the rocky knoll below the Propylaea, Ares, the God of War, was judged by his Olympian peers for the slaying of Poseidon's son. This legendary precedence made the Areopagus, the Hill of Ares, the first court of homicide to which Orestes appealed when pursued by the Furies for the murder of his mother.

Saint Paul preached from this natural pulpit and converted a senator who was canonized and as Saint Dionysius the Areopagite became the patron of Athens.

## THE PNYX

On this hill all citizens, 18,000 in the Golden Age, sat as the Popular Assembly approving or rejecting the laws "tightly crowded together", hence the name Pnyx. From the rostrum cut into the rock the orators - Solon, Themistocles, Pericles and Demosthenes - but also a much larger number of demagogues harangued the Athenians in the first attempt at direct democracy.

*The Bema in the Pnyx*

*Pericles addressing the Athenians on the hill of Pnyx*

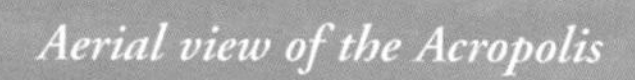

*Aerial view of the Acropolis*

# THE ANCIENT AGORA OF ATHENS

The remains of the ancient Agora are dominated by the restored Stoa of Attalus. This market place was the centre of public life, but also the hub of the principal urban roads and country highways. The long colonnades offered shade in summer and protection from rain in winter to the throng of people who transacted the government of the city or their own business. Not that things spiritual were ever missing from daily life in Athens; under the same marble arches Socrates and Plato instructed their pupils, Zeno expounded the philosophy of the stoics, imitated by envious sophists.

The excavation of the Agora was carried out by the American School of Classical Studies, after the expropriation and destruction of a whole district which had encroached and gradually covered the entire site. The foundations of the main buildings are still easily distinguished; the circular Tholos was the principal centre of executive power and administration, but also the repository of standard measures and weights. The 500 senators met in the Bouleuterion to deliberate on the laws to be submitted to the Popular Assembly; long stone slabs inscribed with decrees and legal texts have come to light. The Metroon, a vast building of complex structure, was the Sanctuary of the Great Mother, the deity of the pre-Hellenic settlers, who had somehow become associated with the Olympian gods; the state archives were kept in adjacent rooms. A small marble slab, once again stands before the Tholos and bears the inscription "I am the boundary of the Agora" to remind citizens to bear themselves with due dignity. There were several other temples, to Ares, Apollo and to the 12 gods collectively, but the characteristic element of the Agora was the stoa, the colonnade which fulfilled both practical and decorative purposes. They surrounded the market in various styles and sizes, and one of them has been faithfully reconstructed by the American School of Classical Studies. It was originally built by Attalus, King of Pergamus in the second century B.C. as a tribute of gratitude to the culture of Athens where he had received his education. The two superimposed galleries contained 21 shops on each floor, flanked respectively by Doric and Ionian columns, but are now the Agora museum for the vases and sculptures found on the site.

*The remains of the ancient agora and the Stoa of Attalus in the backround*

*The temple of Hephaestus (Theseion)*

## THE TEMPLE OF HEPHAESTUS

This Doric temple by Ictinos, the architect of the Parthenon, was known for centuries as the Theseion, because the frieze depicts the exploits and adventures of Theseus. It is now known to have been dedicated to Hephaestus, god of blacksmiths and potters, whose forges and workshops have been located in this quarter since antiquity. Constructed in the fifth century B.C., this is the best-preserved Greek temple, and its 34 columns still support the original roof.

Consecrated to Saint George in the 6th century, it was used as a mosque by the Turks and served later as a burial ground for foreign Protestants.

*The temple of Hephaestus (Theseion)*

*The Tower of the winds*

## THE ROMAN AGORA - TOWER OF THE WINDS

The Emperor Augustus built the four-pillared gate to the Roman Agora which Hadrian surrounded with marble colonnades. The 1st century B.C. Tower of the Winds was a gift of Andronicus Cyrrhestes, a hydraulic clock with a sun dial and weather vane, believed by the Turks to be the tomb of two local prophets, Socrates and Plato, and thus protected and guarded by dervishes.

The form of the marble octagon corresponds to the eight winds, whose symbolic winged figures are represented on the frieze.

*The Arch of Hadrian*

## THE ARCH OF HADRIAN

The slender arch consisting of an apsis decorated with Corinthian columns proclaims on the western side "This is the city of Theseus" and on the eastern "This is the city of Hadrian". Hadrian indeed greatly enlarged the town and established entire new quarters north of the temple of Zeus.

## THE TEMPLE OF ZEUS

Hadrian completed the temple of Olympian Zeus about 700 years after Peisistratus had raised the first immense columns - 7 feet 10 inches in diameter. The 104 Corinthian marble columns of the Roman sanctuary were a third smaller, though still the largest in Europe, as was the temple itself, 354 by 135 feet. The Roman general Sulla removed the pillars of the intervening Hellenistic temple to Rome in the first century B.C.; Genoese and Venetians did likewise with Hadrian's marbles, so that only 16 columns now remain, 13 standing together under their architraves.

*The Temple of Olympian Zeus*

# DIPYLON - KERAMEICOS

The Dipylon was Athens' principal gate, a rectangular court between the potters' quarter where the famous Attican vases were made, and the official cemetery after it became fashionable in the 7th century B.C. to be buried outside the walls. The Sacred Gate nearby gave access to the Sacred Way to Eleusis, and round it some parts of Themistocles' hastily constructed wall, in the face of Spartan objections, are still discernible.

The alley leading from the Sacred Way into the "Potters' field" is lined with interesting memorials to the dead, mostly variations on the farewell theme, though there were also magnificent sepulchral monuments to Athens' greatest sons, as for instance Cleisthenes and Pericles. The latter delivered here his famous speech for the Athenians fallen in the first year of the Peloponnesian War, one of the greatest pieces of oratory as recorded by Thucydides. A charging bull is one of the most striking but also unusual be memorials.

During succeeding ages a series of cemeteries were superimposed on the antique resting place, which was only uncovered in 1861 during the construction of the road linking the capital with its port. The outstanding finds have been removed to the Archaeological Museum, but several 6th-century tombstones including some bas-reliefs of outstanding artistic value are exhibited in the local museum. Especially noteworthy is the funerary stela of Dexileos, aide-de-camp to the commander in the Corinthian War, who was killed at the age of twenty.

Next to the Dipylon built by Lycurgus in the 4th century B.C. was the Pompeion, the depot for the paraphernalia used for religious celebrations and starting point of the Panathenaean procession.

*The stele of Hegeso in Kerameikos Cemetery*

*The alles of tombs in the outer Kerameikos*

## THE MONUMENT OF PHILOPAPPUS

The highest hill (482 feet) facing the Acropolis is crowned by the ruined marble monument of Philopappus, a Syrian prince and Roman consul, honoured by the Athenians in 116 A.D. for his gifts to their city. One of the caves below is supposedly the prison of Socrates, where the greatest of ancient philosophers drained the fatal cup of hemlock.

## THE MONUMENT OF LYSICRATES

This 4th-century B.C. choragic monument, one of many that once lined the street of the Tripods from the town to the theatre of Dionysus, owes its preservation to the fact that it served from 1669 till the 19th century as library of the French Capuchin monastery, where Byron stayed during his first visit and where he wrote his famous poem "Maid of Athens". The tiny cylindrical edifice of Pentelic marble rises 21 feet above its base. The frieze depicts the defeat of the Tyrrhenian pirates by Dionysus.

*The monument of Lysicrates* *The monument of Philopappus*

*National Archeol. Museum. Harper. Cycladic art (2400-2200 B.C.)*

## THE NATIONAL ARCHAEOLOGICAL MUSEUM

This is one of the world's great collections of sculptures and vases, covering the full range of almost 3000 years of ancient Greek civilization, continued by representative works of the Hellenistic and Roman period and some splendid Byzantine jewellery. The collection was started before Greek independence had yet become a reality, and thus antedates the building of the museum. Valuable gifts, like the Karapanos finds, which occupies a whole gallery with the excavations from Dodona and Corfu, and the Stathatos collection of small archaic bronzes, vases and especially splendid gold ornaments from the 12th century B.C. to the Byzantine period, have been added, but new significant finds constantly enrich this unparalleled artistic treasure.

Schliemann's excavations in the 1870's contributed the unique Mycenaean Treasure, gold masks covering the faces of the dead, ornaments, vessels and weapons of exquisite design and craftsmansip. Another important discovery of diadems, gold cups and a magnificent crystal bowl was made in Mycenae in 1952, but other Bronze Age palaces all over Greece likewise yield up ever new treasure troves.

Archaic sculpture is represented by the kouroi, statues of nude youths standing with the left foot advanced and hands pressed to their side. To one of these belonged the head of a young man found in the Ceramicus. Of the same period are the colossal Apollo and the equally large Dioscuri.

Classical mastery in the handling of movement reached perfection in "Poseidon about to throw the Trident" and a delightful bronze race horse with its Jockey boy, retrieved like so many of the bronze statues from the sea near the coast and islands.

The wealth of ex-voto and funerary stelae is unsurpassed. Some of the finest come from the Ceramicus, including works by the eminent 4th-century B.C. sculptor Scopas, but the outstanding bas-relief is closely connected with the Eleusinian cult, showing Demeter handing Triptolemus the first seed of corn.

The entire second floor is given over to ceramics, from the hand-made vessels with austere geometric drawings of the early Aegean period to the decorative maritime designs of the Mycenaean period (1600 - 1100 B.C.), the oriental richness of Archaic times (700 - 550 B.C.) to culminate in the elegant sophistication of the Attic vases, black figures in the 6th century B.C., red figures in the next, and some rare 4th-century B.C. lecythoi with polychrome figures on a white background. Equally rich is the display of figurines, from the stiff stylised 8th-century B.C. horses to the flowing drapery of the charming Tanagra ladies of the 4th century B.C.

The numismatic section displays over 250,000 coins from their clumsy European beginning in Aegina in the 6th century B.C. to the superbly executed classical and Hellenistic 'pieces to end with the shoddy specimens of the declining Byzantine Empire.

*Mask from the Acropolis of Mycenae (middle of 2nd millennium B.C.)*

*National Archeol. Museum - The Cup from Vafio*

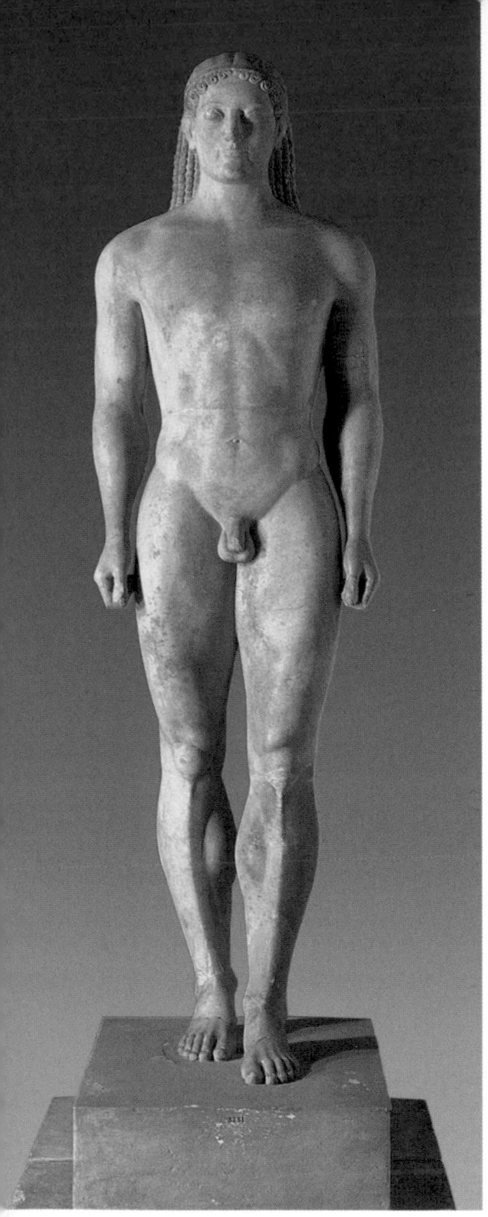

*National Archeol. Museum*
*Statue of youth (Kouros) from Anavyssos*
*(About 550 B.C.)*

*National Archeol. Museum*
*Big funerary ampfora of the ripe geometric style*
*(about 800 B.C.)*

*National Archeol. Museum. Bronze race horse with its small Jockey. Found in 1927 of Cape Artemision in Euboea. About the middle of the 2nd century B.C*

*The bronze statue of Athena*

*The Youth of Antikythera*

*National Archeol. Museum. Aphrodite, Pan Eros*

*National Archeol. Museum. Bronze statue of Poseidon (or Zeus) 460 B.C.*

## BYZANTINE ATHENS

During the 700 years of Byzantine rule Athens declined in inverse ratio to the growth of Constantinople. Hadrian's lavish building activities had endowed Athens with a wealth of sacred and profane edifices, which more than sufficed for the needs of a dwindling, impoverished population. The transformation of the temples into churches enabled the Athenians to continue their worship in the familiar surroundings, but by the 10th century the depleted congregations felt lost in the spacious magnificence of the past. Several tiny churches in the traditional Byzantine plan of "cross in square" under a dome resting on an octagonal drum proved that loss of size is not necessarily accompanied by loss in taste.

Aghios Nicodemos, the oldest and largest, rises above the ruins of a Roman bath. The architectural purity has been maintained despite the lavish 19th-century decorations of the interior. The 11th-century Panaghia Kapnikarea (Our Lady of the Smoke) was originally a minute basilica in plan, later enlarged to the Greek cross. The custom of offering bridal wreaths to the virgin Athena has here been continued to the Virgin Mary.

The 12th-century Aghios Eleutherios likewise connects with an older worship, that of Eleutho, goddess of child-bearing, which accounts for the second dedication to Panaghia Gorgoepikoos (Our Lady of Urgent Requests). The archbishops officiated in this miniature metropolis for many centuries after the Turkish occupation. Built in the beautifully matured marble walls are classical fragments, a frieze of the Attic festal calendar, bas-reliefs of symbolic beasts and heraldic designs.

Earlier the Orthodox archbishops had their throne in the 12th-century Panaghia Sotira (Our Lady of Salvation) near the Tower of the Winds, after their expulsion from the Parthenon by the Franks. Too big to be left to the Christians, it was converted into a Turkish mosque, degraded to a military bakery before being ultimately restored to

*The Byzantine Church of Saint Eleutherios*

*The Byzantine Church of Kapnikarea*

the Virgin.

With the exception of the 11th-century Omorphi Ecclesia (Pretty Church) with an unusual high octagonal dome and lovely 16th-century frescoes, all the other Byzantine gems are crowded within the narrow limits of the medieval town below the Acropolis. Aghios Ioannis Kolonna (Saint John of the Column) is a singlenaved basilica constructed round a Roman column which projects above the roof and to which prayers are still tied as at the earlier pagan shrine, several of whose pillars stand before the entrance.

The 11th-century revival under the Macedonian dynasty also produced Aghioi Apostoloi above the Agora, Aghioi Assomatoi (All Souls) near the Theseion, and Panaghia (Our Lady) on Monastiraki Square opposite the only mosque built as such and not converted from Christianity.

At the confines of the district is Aghioi Theodoroi, to whose delicate 11th-century brick-and-stone work a terracotta frieze was added in the 15th century.

*Byzantine Museum: Icon of the archangel Michael (14th sentury)*

*The Monastery of Kaissariani*

## THE MONASTERY OF KAISSARIANI

Of the five monasteries on Mount Hymettus, the retreat of Kaissariani - though long disaffected - is by far the most romantic. Built on a sanctuary of Aphrodite near a spring, the 11$^{th}$-century hexagonal cupola supported by four Ionian columns blends harmoniously with the later narthex and campanile. The 16$^{th}$-century frescoes portray the Virgin seated between the Archangels in the apse and the Apostles on the north wall.

The refectory, kitchen and some cells have been restored in the charming setting of the wooded slopes.

*The Byzantine Monastery of Daphni*

## DAPHNI

The Emperor Justinian constructed a fortified monastery over the ruined temple of Apollo, but the church of the Assumption with its magnificent mosaics was only added some 500 years later. The Frankish dukes invited Cistercian monks as guardians of their last resting place and two sarcophagi with fleurs-de-lis still stand in the Gothic cloisters.

When the last duke strangled his aunt before Daphni's altar, Sultan Mohammed II occupied Athens, executed the duke and expelled the Cistercians. After centuries of neglect Orthodox monks returned and defended the monastery during the War of Independence. Following extensive restorations the superb mosaic of Christ Pantocrator looks again severaly down on biblical scenes of astounding freedom of line and delicate colouring.

*The Christ Pantocrator in the vault of the Church of Daphni (11th cent)*

## MODERN ATHENS

The centre is Constitution Square below the former royal palace which was finished in time for King Otho to grant there the constitution that delayed his fall for 20 years; but after the revolution of 1923 which overthrew King George II it became the parliament. In the retaining walls of the palace ramp are the marble and bronze bas-reliefs of the Tomb of the Unknown Soldier. The Royal Garden extending to Hasdrian's arch was Queen Amalia's most praiseworthy contribution to Otho's reign.

Since the restoration of 1935 the kings have resided in the smaller residence built by the German Ernest Ziller in the Renaissance style of the 1890's. All around rise tall apartment blocks, as luxurious as any in Europe, though in the main thoroughfare of this fashionable district, Queen Sophia Avenue, some of the 19th-century embassies have remained unaltered, but overshadowed by the ultramodern American Embassy, the Hilton and the Megaron Moussikis.

Below Constitution Square (Syntagma) extends the main shopping quarter on both sides of Hermes Street, appropriately called after the god of trade. Two main roads connect Constitution Square with Athens' second, more popular heart, Concord Square (Omonia). In Venizelos Avenue stands Schliemann's Palace of Ilion, now seat of the Supreme Court, followed by the Roman Catholic Cathedral of Saint Dionysius the Areopagite, the neo-Byzantine eye-hospital and the imposing neo-classical Academy, University and National Library.

The centre of Concord Square covers the main station of the Piraeus-Kifissia electric railway and Attico Metro. Patission Street leads north, past the neo-classical Polytechnic School and Archaeological Museum to King Constantine's equestrian statue at the entrance of the Mars Field. Higher up rises a pillar topped by a helmeted Britannia, the British Commonwealth war memorial.

These are the landmarks of the sprawling metropolis

*The Greek Parliament in Constsitution Square. (Syntagma)*

*The Academy, the University and the National Library in Panepistimiou street*

into which the modest city, whose plan was drawn up jointly by the Greek Cleanthes and the German Schaubert, has grown in a hundred and thirty years. Both architects were called by King Otho from Berlin and given a house in the Plaka district in which the newly founded University was provisionally installed. Cleanthes designed the palace of the Duchesse de Plaisance, now the Byzantine Museum, a splendid collection of icons, wood carvings and embroideries. He also built the pseudo-Norman English church, while Schaubert was responsible for the large Orthodox cathedral and the reconstruction of the temple of Athena Nike.

*Evzones (Presidential Guard) at the monument of the unknown Soldier*

*The Academy of Athens*

## BUILDINGS IN NEO - CLASSIC STYLE
## THE STADIUM

The Royal Palace contains the earliest elements of neoclassicism, but this style came to full flowering in the three centres of Greek cultural life on Venizelos Avenue, planned by the Danish Hansen brothers and paid for by the munificence of the Greco-Austrian Baron Sina. The marble colonnade and pediment of the Academy are flanked by two tall columns bearing the statues of Athena and Apollo, the University is preceded by a painted colonnade, while the National Library is faced with a Doric portico. Theophil Hansen also designed the exhibition hall in the Zappeion Garden.

Fitted into a natural ravine of the pine-clad Ardettus hill, the 70,000-seat stadium was laid out by Lycurgus in the 4th century B.C., covered with dazzling white Pentelic marble by Herodes Atticus some 500 years later, and completely restored by the modern benefactor Averoff in time for the revived Olympic Games in 1896.

*The Panathenaic Stadium*

*The Athens Olympic Stadium during the olympic games in 2004*

*The temple of Zeus and the Acropolis in the background*

*Acropolis View from the north-west with mount Hymettus in the background*

## ATHENS THE GREAT CITY

Before exploring the vast and varied conglomeration of Greater Athens it might be advisable to study the lie of the town from the height of the Acropolis or even better from Mount Lycabettus round which modern districts of tall white blocks of flats extend in all directions. A funicular railway leads to the chapel of St. George on the barren top from which the unimpeded view opens East and South to the sea, North, and West to the semicircle formed by Mount Hymettus, Mount Pentelicon, scarred by marble quarries, the green peaks of Mount Parnese and low barren Mount Aegaleon, a vast expanse of houses diminishing in height towards the periphery and broken by parks and gardens.

*Part of central Athens with Mt. Lycavittos in the background*

## PLAKA - THE OLD CITY

Several minute Byzantine chapels are tucked away in the Plaka district on the northern and eastern slope of the Acropolis, corresponding roughly in size to the wretched village enclosed within a wall that became in 1834 King Otho's capital and was in the following thirty years rebuilt in the style still named after him.

The narrow lanes have preserved their characteristic local colour, though at night echoing to the music of guitars and larger orchestras as the one - or two - storeyed houses now all accommodate tourist and popular taverns, night clubs and bars. Gaiety reaches a crowded climax each carnival which Athenians like to celebrate all night long in this nostalgic setting.

## PIRAEUS

The Piraeus, connected with Athens by miles of suburbia, is at the same time one of the great emporiums of the Levant as well as the main port and industrial centre of Greece. The harbour and famous Long Walls constructed by Themistocles, the victor of Salamis and creator of the Athenian maritime empire, in the 470's B.C., were pulled down after the defeat in the Peloponnesian War, rebuilt and extended to be destroyed once again by Sulla in the 1st century B.C.. The Piraeus never fully recovered till the foundation of the Greek Kingdom in the 19th century, when its natural advantages and proximity to the capital gradually transformed a desolate fishing village into one of the busiest ports in the Mediterranean, crowded with passenger liners and freighters flying the flags of all nations.

The main harbour is at its most picturesque on January 6, Epiphany, when the Blessing of the Waters is celebrated with great pomp, attended by representatives of the Government.

The smaller vessels of antiquity weres heltered in two well-protected basins opening south and separated by a precipitous headland. At Zea the slipways of the ancient triremes are still discernible in the rock, but enlarged by a new breakwater it is now the leading European yacht harbour. The crescent-shaped waterfront is lined with open-air cafes to the western end above which lie the remains of the Hellenistic theatre and the interesting museum. On the top of the steep hill on the Eastern promontory ancient drama is performed in a new amphitheatre against the incomparable backdrop of the Saronic Gulf and Mount Hymettus.

The Royal Yacht Club below dominates the ancient port of Mounychia, now known as Tourcolimano, crowded with brightly coloured fishing boats. The fishermen mending their nets add a touch of the islands, while the restaurants which border the seashore are famous for their seafood.

*The Port of Piraeus*

*The picturesque Mikrolimano*

*The Vouliagmeni Beach*

## THE APOLLO COAST
## PHALERON - GLYFADA - VOULIAGMENI - LAGONISSI

The four straight miles of Syngrou Avenue join Athens to the sea and the coastal road which extends for 44 miles from Tourcolimano to Cape Sounion, along the popular beaches framed by innumerable restaurants, taverns, night clubs and bars. Through Old Phaleron, past Elleniko and the Youth Sport Centre of Aghios Kosmas to Glyfada, an elegant resort where some of the best hotels and places of entertainment are situated.

At Voula the foothills of Hymettus come down to the beach installations which link with the wooded Kavouri headland. Vouliagmeni is a particularly attractive holiday choice, with two fine sandy beaches, a pine-clad promontory, yacht harbour and a sulphurous lake whose water possesses well-known curative qualities, while the picturesque overhanging cliffs provide a lovely setting for theatrical performances on the floating stage.

The lonely splendour of the Apollo Coast is emphasized by the undulating hills fragrant with thyme and wild flowers, the crystal clear sea from which enchanting islets rise close to the shore. Past the excellent beach of Varkisa to Lagonissi, a self-contained bungalow village to Anavyssos with its vast salt pans and glittering mountains of salt.

## KIFISSIA - MARATHON - MOUNT PARNESE

The garden suburb of Kifissia lies in the foothills of mount Pentelicon, pleasantly cool even in the hot summer. The road continues through pine forests to the large artificial lake of Marathon, held back by the only marble dam in the world. In the luxuriant vegetation below the 932ft-wide and 236ft-high white wall stands a replica of the 5th-century B.C. Athenian Treasury at Delphi.

Much closer to the North coast rises the 39ft-high tumulus erected over the ashes of the 192 Athenians who gave their lives at the battle of Marathon, thus saving their town and perhaps Europe. Miltiades conceived the daring plan of strengthening the wings of his 10,000 Athenians to envelop and destroy the Persian centre. The messenger sent to Athens expired after announcing the sensational victory, but the Marathon Race is still an endurance test at sporting events.

Mount Parnese is the most formidable of the three mountain ranges which ring Athens. Among the alpine scenery on its upper slopes, where fir trees replace the Attic pine, snow makes skiing possible all through the winter. Aghios Merkourios in the lower reaches is surrounded by gentle meadows and woods.

*The Tymvos of Marathon*

*Sounion - The temple of Poseidon*

## SOUNION - TEMPLE OF POSEIDON

The wind-swept cape was an obvious choice for a sanctuary of Poseidon, where the sailors might offer a last sacrifice to propitiate the mighty God of the Sea, before leaving the comparative safety of the Saronic Gulf for the perils of the open archipelago. The archaic temple was destroyed by the Persians in 480 B.C. and rebuilt like numerous other shrines throughout Attica by Pericles. The pure whiteness of the 12 remaining Doric columns is still as dazzling against the deep-blue sky as in the days of Byron who carved his name into the marble.

On a lower hill, beyond the fortifications of the Peloponnesian War, stands the temple of Athena Sounias, a simple rectangle to which Ionian colonnades were later added on two sides.

The barren cliffs become even more grandiose, the seascape expands and the southernmost tip of Attica, Cape Sounion, points at an arc of islands.

*Cape Sounion. The temple of Poseidon*

*Sounion. Sunset over the temple of Poseidon*